# 21st-Century

# *Psalms of*

# DAVID

## DAVID LORANG

ISBN 978-1-63961-250-5 (paperback)
ISBN 978-1-63961-251-2 (digital)

Christian Faith Publishing, Inc.
832 Park Avenue
Meadville, PA 16335
www.christianfaithpublishing.com

Printed in the United States of America

# *Everlasting Bridge*

F or as the dawn breaks, the stars and the moon and all the trees were put in order for us to enjoy. For the Lord has built a bridge that stretches to the heavens. A bridge that can never be torn down. A bridge that never rusts away, that never deteriorates, and that needs no maintenance. A permanent bridge. Greater than any bridge that a man could build. That bridge is Jesus Christ, the foundation to heaven's door, a passageway to eternal life where there are no tears, there is no sickness, no disease, and no anxiety—a place where only joy remains, a place where you will go. As you travel on the bridge of life in Christ, there are obstacles, there are potholes, and there are places that we can detour; but stay steadfast and stay on the bridge. For that bridge is the only one or thing that can take you to a place that has no pain. So today as the dawn breaks or as the sun fades away, remember Jesus Christ is with you and will never forsake you. As for me, I will stay steadfast on that bridge that takes us to heaven's gates. If you see anyone off this bridge, restore them with love.

# Holding All the Cards

If we find love inside ourselves, we hold all the cards in this life and the next. Nothing can be taken from you. If we hold and trust, then we will have peace. If we hold Jesus Christ, then we hold all the cards. If we are slow to speak, we will hear the whisper through the dark. That will bring us to the still place in our minds. Even when He was nailed to the cross, He held all the cards. Even when King David spent fifteen years or more in the wilderness, he held all the cards. So hold all the cards today, and you will find your way through the dark. Love is Christ Jesus, and He accepts all people but not sin, so read His word and love on. Hold all the cards, and the Son of God is with you.

# To the Women of Christ

Her beauty is like the stars in the heavens. Her love is like the depths of the oceans. Her eyes are as clear as the Lord's love is to my heart at Calvary. Her love covers me as a blanket on a cold night. Her voice is like a choir of angels singing to the Lord Jesus Christ in the dead of night. Her words are like the hand of Christ giving life as He carved her out of solid diamonds and pearls. Her skin is like solid gold. Her love for Jesus Christ stretches to the heavens and encompass all who hear and see her. Her touch is as loving as dove on the morning sunrise. She seeks after peace, hope, and love in Christ, like it is solid gold. She seeks after the will of our Father and righteousness for His namesake. This is all the women in Christ. So lay down your life for Christ, and you will start to see Christ in her eyes, touch, and love that comes from the Father. All tenderness that she gives you is the Father's love at the cross. To the wife you have or the wife that is to come, cover her with the love that pass all understanding, and you will see her beauty as Christ sees her as a star that burns in His heart and to the heavens.

# *Counterfeit*

F or there are many original things. There is a real pair of Oakley's or a cheap knockoff, a real Picasso or a Leo deviance. For there are also imitators. Just ask yourself if you want something fake that looks good or you want the real McCoy. When God speaks, the earth shakes and hope is here for all; and if the devil speaks, only confusion and disappointment and death come from his words. It is like a fire that's producing nothing but ash. But then Christ will bring his city out of the ashes and put His foot upon Satan's head, and Christ will put the devil out of our perspective forever more and peace will rain in our hearts minds and life as I should have.

So do you want the King of peace or king of sin or just counterfeit? Seek Christ, and life is at your door and the counterfeit will be no more.

# A Song to Myself

I love honesty even if it's not what I want to hear. As long as it's in love so I can hear the truth of His will. Love Christ for His truth is the love I always need. He holds my heart and hopes and forms me with His tender hands. As I hold His word in my heart, it always finds a way to soften my understanding and gives me hope. Even though I can't always understand His ways, I accept them by faith. It is not by my own understanding but by His grace. In His time, the Lord sings His song in my heart so I can sing His song in this dark world. No one can see my song if I keep it to myself. Christ is the best thing for mankind—the gateway to the song maker.

PS: Thank you, Father, for Christ and the song in my heart.

# Always Remember

You are sealed by the Holy Spirit, by the truth of Christ, and by the power of His understanding. At times, we must accept these things by faith and not by our own minds until the power of Christ's revelation comes to us. For the Holy Spirit is our translator of the word of the living God. Always remember it is written, "I Am who I Am." Christ is alive through the Holy Spirit. But if you do not know His word, it is awfully hard to hear Christ speaking to you or if your understanding is from just somebody else's relationship. The Lord is calling us deeper so you can truly understand peace, hope, and joy. And all are called to give their selves freely to Christ, and you will not be disappointed in the fruit of your life. Always remember peace and joy only flow from Jesus Christ. His love never departs from us. We just have a hard time seeing in the darkness of our understanding of his word. Faith, hope, and love always remain. If the earth were just a football field closer to the sun or a city block away, we would all be dead. Do not put your hope in science, but put it in the science of common sense. It takes more faith to believe in a lie than the truth that is in our life in Christ. Always remember to hold love and peace, to all and yourself in Christ.

# Anger

As hope is found in Christ, His love will never run dry if we hold His Son in our hearts, mind, and life. When we fall short, He will redeem it for our good. If we hold love, then anger will not be on our lips much. As for me, Christ is the love that keeps my anger at bay, in my mouth, heart, and life. The Lord is slow to anger as we should be, so our responses will be measured as Christ sees fit. Anger is not a tool we should be in when sin is in our hearts. Even Jesus only got angry a few times in His life by his action with religious people, profiting on His church or people. The Lord will not put out a smoking flax. So we must not use anger in our hearts, mind, and actions to take people out of Christ. Anger in sin is death to us all. If you hold Christ and, anger will not find a place in our hearts. Christ is like the most powerful superhero you could ever have in your heart, mind, and actions. So when we use anger, let love be in our heart and our actions. So we do not lose one soul to the lie of this age. Let's walk, not run, in His wholeness, and anger can be far from our lips. When you see others pray and give love with truth, your words will be like gold to their ears. And Christ will fill your heart with love, peace, and truth in His living word. Anger will submit to Christ, and every knee will bow to our King of Kings. God does not judge in your anger but in your love. He sent his only Son, Christ, who is our hope against anger.

# Be a People Pleaser Today

Deny your body is denying Christ's greatest creation. We are made in His image, according to His likeness. We are the apple of His eyes. When we read the scripture for the first time, we have the surface of the word in our understanding and our relationship with Christ. Let's go deeper and be a people pleaser in Christ. Let's please people by pleasing Christ first, by walking in the fruits of the Spirit—love, self-control, and long-suffering. Now we cannot do this on our own. We must stand in His word until He goes deeper in our understanding. If we continue to repeat the scripture in our mind over and over, and no peace comes, we are holding the scripture in our image. We must hold His living word in His image for breakthrough, healing, peace, and self-control. Do not become the accuser to yourself or others at all costs. I am a recovering people pleaser, and then I hold His living word in His image, and the peace of Christ is in my mind and life. So be a people pleaser today by honoring your commitment to Christ, not to people.

When we are overwhelmed or covered in confusion each day, we are not caring about His yoke. His yoke is easy. Christ only had a three-year ministry; it's not about the quantity but the quality of the fruit of the Spirit. You are right where Christ needs you. Sometimes, an apple looks really good, but it tastes very bad. So let's strike a balance to where Christ is moving you, and you will be a true people pleaser of God's living word. Only Christ can truly please people, so hold Him to find the way out of confusion and pain. He is the light of the world and the light in you. So who are you pleasing today? He will add to you as He sees fit. Hold love, and you will be a true people pleaser. If we hold love in His image, then peace He will leave with us. Give peace in the dark today, and you are in the Father's hands.

# Church of Freedom

Calling to all, calling to you, calling to all denominations and churches. Calling to drinkers, calling to liars, calling to people trapped in the sin of the body. To all who do not fit into the church of judgment and who can't go even on Sunday or rather spend time with their family and friends on Wednesday. Call to all who want Jesus Christ, not religion. Call to the women who had abortions. To men who talk like a sailor. Calling to you who do not want or feel you can't give 10 percent of your money. Who just wants a place to come and be with God? Calling to all. To the man who lives with his girlfriend. To the man who loves beer more than life itself. Calling to preachers and teachers of Christ. Calling to all. This is a church of freedom. Where all are welcome if you smoke; gamble; or use methamphetamines, heroin, and cocaine. This is a church of deliverance. If you do not know all the church lingo or how to pray or sing, if you just want a place to come and listen, this is a church of freedom, a place to come as you are. Let God do His work in our life. Calling to you. Calling to all who can't find peace. This is a church of freedom in you and a church of the living God. Christ is with us all. If your church has Christ, then it can be the church of freedom. Just do not stand on people but stand on Christ, not sin. This is a church of freedom. The Lord will destroy man's image of the church and continue to build it in His image. Christ is the church of freedom.

# *Consequences*

In this life, there are many consequences. Some consequences are good or bad. Sometimes you do the right thing, and the consequences in this life do not work out. You can do the wrong thing in this life and get rewarded for it. True success is being close to Christ and being where He wants you even if you die or do not look successful in man's eyes. The consequence of not being with Christ is dying in this life and the next. So stay close to His living word, and allow the Holy Spirit to teach you. When I am writing, I just try to stay out of His way. So the Lord knows all things. His ways are far above ours. The real true consequence is failing to do the right thing that's morally pleasing to Christ in your heart and life. If we look to please our family, friends, or colleagues outside God's will, we all lose. You can see if somebody is missing a leg or arm. It makes it harder for that person and others who love them. We must not lose any part of Christ's body because it will make it just a little harder for us all. Calling to you who want the true consequence of Christ to burn in your heart like a star that never burns out. For, in the end, you and Christ will stand before God; and you must settle in your heart and life. Who will you please today?

The true consequence is not running to the Father, Son, and Holy Spirit. All greatness in you and this world is His. The only thing that Christ can*not* do is sin. And we are knitted in sin. Our only hope is in Christ. Do not hide from him in the storm of your own mind or life today. Find the true consequences that bring hope, peace, and love, and the greatest is love. Then it will overflow to all people in your life, and we all need those consequences.

# Deeper in Christ

If we want to go deeper, we must learn to be just a little simpler. Childlike faith, not trying to understand everything. No matter how much a bird would like to understand this world, it's just out of its reach. We need to trust that God's understanding is just out of reach at times in our life. So let's go deeper and hold Christ today. Let's not have too much knowledge of God's living word. Let's have more faith and stillness in His word, and we will be deeper in Christ. Let's think and love like a child because that is what we are in the Father's eyes. So let's light up our Father's eyes by loving one another with His living word. Do not twist or distort the unity of Christ to fulfill our own churches' will. We do not need to stand on one another to go deeper in Christ. Speak the truth in love and long-suffering by loving one another, and you will be deeper in Christ.

# Do Not Listen to Me

We who know the truth know when to speak and when to listen. We who have Christ have the truth. We just have to hear Him, whispering through the sin of our minds at times. It is written that we were knitted in our mother's womb in sin. So it takes time to hear the whisper through the dark. We must learn to take part in the spirit of Christ in our mind, heart, and life. Remember it did not take one day for you to get where you are in your heart, mind, and life. So do not listen to me in this life. Hear Christ and His teachings in your mind, heart, and life.

Humbleness is not just something that comes out of our mouths. It's something Christ has to work on us and in us. You have to find your own way to hear Christ in your mind, heart, and life. Do not listen to me but to Him through me. Calling to all. Calling to you to listen to the voice of Jesus Christ in you and from others. Who can truly see yourself without Christ? So we must learn to listen to Him through others and our self. Just remember He had to talk out of jackass in the word of God. Let's not let it get that far today. So do not listen to me. Find Christ within your heart, mind, and in my words today, and make sure you are not listening to me but Christ in you.

# *Fighting*

Only the Son of God has the power to forgive sin; if you know it, you can speak, and it brings you peace in each word. If it's a lie, it will torment your mind, heart, and life. Do not fight one to another with words but fight with love, peace, and self-control. Do not try to do it alone, even Christ had someone with Him when He was doing the Father's work in other people. We must stay in church, family, and with friends who fill us with hope in our hearts, mind, and life. You have peace, hope, and love when you hold Christ. So fight with all of the fruits of the spirit, and your fight will be in peace.

Mark 2:13–15

# *Find Your Beauty in the Cross*

Find your beauty on the cross. The world builds up itself in its money, lust, and all the pleasures mankind. But in the end, they are emptier than when they started. If you look for peace in money or lust of the flesh, then you are not getting what you want, and your peace has been taken. So do not look for temporary things of this world. Look for Christ, and He will fill your beauty at the cross of Calvary. You will find your true beauty in body, mind, and life. As each day comes, put your beauty on the cross of hope, peace, and love. Your beauty cannot be lost in Christ. As the blood of Christ covers your life, you will start to see the beauty of our cross, and hope in Christ has been put in us all.

Do not fear the storms on the horizon. Not even death can take you from the beauty in the cross even the Son of God had to die. Be like a child. We can accept the truth that you will never die as long as you hold the beauty in the cross of Christ. If you are hearing Christ in this writing, the beauty of the cross is within your life, and nothing will be lost. Faith is from heaven, and only Christ can open our spiritual eyes to the beauty in the cross. Thanks be to Christ our creator. You are beautiful just as you are at the cross of Calvary.

# Good Shepherd

S ometimes I look into my heart, and I do not see Christ. But I'm just wanting things for myself, and I feel I am back at the beginning. Nothing that makes my heart more broken than not staying in His word, and it brings me sadness that I would stray from the good shepherd. Then I seek Jesus Christ, and He restores my faith and my trust that He is in control of my heart, mind, and life. When my heart is not good, Christ is bigger than my heart and that brings me great joy and hope in the good shepherd of my heart, mind, and life. When we find ourself outside of His green pastures, know we all fall short in our minds, heart, and life at times. The good shepherd will take us from the crooked places and give us joy, peace, and hope through His living word in our life. My good shepherd is Jesus Christ; He lives on the inside of my heart and life. If you do not know the good shepherd, just call on Christ, and He will come and make your crooked places straight through people who know love, peace, and self-control in His living word. I have a good shepherd who will never die. Hope is on the way to you.

# Grow

As we grow in Christ, we must look back at His life and all the mighty men and women of His living word. Read His Word, and let Christ find you where you are today. Do not allow religious lies to come into your life, mind, or heart. It's not just about the outward acts of our faith. It's truly about both. The work of God's word takes time. Christ is in your life. The Lord wants to give you more than a mouth that worships our Lord and Christ but a life of hope in your mind and life even when you are growing. When we grow, that is Christ in you where money, sex, and fame will not control you; but you will control the tools of our dark mind and world by reading and staying in the Lord's plan for you. And the only way is for Christ to change us on the inside. So allow the Holy Spirit to lead us out of the dark together. Now that takes time to grow out of the darkness of our mind and life. The light we need to grow is Christ so get close to Christ in your mind and life then you will grow in His light. Hold on to God's living word when life is slow or fast. Hope is found at the place you are in Christ. Just as you know that a tree is growing, if you stand there all day, you will not see it grow. Just as you are growing, sometimes it's hard to see. If you are reading this today, you are growing. Trust Christ, not yourself, and you will grow today. Have faith in your life in Christ. You cannot see the wind, but you know it is real. Sometimes we cannot see the growth, but Christ is real and living on the inside of us and our life.

# Hard to Hear

As the day starts, or as the day finishes, it's not by might or by power, but it's by the spirit of the living God. The natural always comes first for us. Let's not be so heavenly minded that we are not earthly good. What God is trying to say to us is that we should pray in all things, hope for all things, and believe in all things; but we must do the natural thing first.

Timothy took some wine for his stomach ailment when Paul encouraged him. We know Paul has faith, so if you're healing has not come yet or never comes, you are having faith. Have faith. Getting what you want is easy, but having faith and not getting what you need in this life is called hard truth or faith. God did not even spare His own Son from death. His thoughts and words can become reality. Nothing can be held back from our God. Death in this life will not destroy you. Do not believe the lie it brings death, but believe or have faith in heaven. All are welcome. The only thing that will be left out is sin. Anything that changes from the Garden of Eden is sin. We cannot find contentment in sexual sin. I know sex makes us feel good, and we were all knitted in our mother's womb in sin. I know we were born with it. But the love of Christ is better than any sin. There is hope for all. Sin is defeated, and you are whole in God through Christ who loves you. Focus on Him, not my words, and it will not be hard to hear.

# He Is the Dream Maker

Find your dream that comes from Christ. Spark your imagination to the dream maker who can put your dreams into reality. Do not hinder the Gospel of Christ by tearing down God's anointed people, and all people are His. Allow Christ to meet them where they are. God is in control of the increase. Do not cause your brother or sister to stumble. If there is smoking flax, continue to lightly blow on it, so you do not blow it out. Then Jesus Christ will bring them deeper in His time. Some plant, some water, the Father can only bring the increases. Always read His word, and walk softly with all God's people, and all is His. Just as you have wrapped around your children's fingers, they have no clue how much you Love them at times. For you are wrapped around the dream makers finger's, and you have no clue how much Christ truly loves you. Just as the sun rises, run to the dream maker, and your dream will be in your sunset. And you will see His love for you. Hold each dream that comes from Christ in your heart, and allow Christ to have His way in your dreams that they may become reality. Or our dream might change. At times, we do not even know our own hearts. So let's trust the dream maker who puts the stars in their place for you and me to enjoy. Run to the dream maker, Christ, today.

# *His Time*

The Lord comes from the least in man's eyes. If you have broken-ness, you have God. If you are self-assured, you have you, not God. We must have Christ to do His will—healing, peace, joy, and contentment in the Holy Spirit. If a man plants ten thousand seeds, and only one is healed or grows, he must see the fruit of his own crop. For the Lord's will is to bear His fruit. So speak the truth in love, and you will have more fruit than you have room for. Let's be led by the Holy Spirit. Let it be His will. If you speak healing, and it comes from Christ, you will see healing. If you see nothing, it is your will at this time. So speak love, truth, and peace to all. In His time, you will see a breakthrough or healing. As Jesus Christ speaks, "I only speak what the Father allows me to speak."

So lay down your will to find His, just as john laid down his will, and his healing was taken, just as Peter healed the lame man. Faith comes from the Father, and we receive it through Christ. Who has done the work for us? So hope and believe in all things so you can be able to walk in where you are until the Father moves your mountain or gives you the grace to accept His will if the mountain does not move. Do not become the accuser to yourself or others. You did have faith because you called on Christ, and you cannot call on Christ if the Father does not open your eyes. Do not lose heart in doing well. Breakthrough is on the way in His time. You are whole as you are in Christ.

We are not in control of much. The Lord picks our sex, our eye color, and our family. So might as well stand still, and let Christ form your life, mind, and in His word. We cannot control God by putting His word in our image or understanding. "I am who I am." The word of God is the written things that He has done. So we must trust in His Love. So we can see the will of Jesus Christ in our life and mind. Then you will walk on water or sleep sound when the storms in your life are raging. So if you would like to help or hold His hand today, you must line up with His will for yourself and others. Let's not pray in a miss. Nothing can be held back from Christ our God. If His will and ours line up, then the works of His hands and yours will have more fruit than you have room for. In His time, we will find His will; so be still in your mind, and walk slowly, and love and peace are on the way.

# *I Am Superior*

If we think or feel we are better or superior to anyone else, we have lost Christ. The Father gives us a measure of faith or an IQ in His word and our understanding. As it is written, "Is a mouth or an eye more important in Christ?" We are all part of God's body and plan. Christ belongs to all—Democrats, Republicans, Independent, and all who have not gotten to know Him. Christ is superior in life and death. The only thing I am superior at is sin. If we build people up in our eyes or expectations, we will not see Christ's works. We will see what our heart wants or thinks it needs from them. The truth is that we all need each other, and Christ is the only one that is superior.

I know it is hard to believe that you need some people. Just remember to set up boundaries in your words, mind, and commitments to others. We do not want to fall into sin in our minds or actions or cause someone else to sin. Christ is the only one who is superior, and He gave His life for us. So lay down your superior mindsets and actions so you can hold Christ the superior one by His grace, not our works. The only thing I am superior at is sin, so I strive to Hold the superior one—Christ.

# You Can

We need to find joy in not having what we want and peace in time we feel lost. The time is now to see true peace in Christ, not in what you have in this life but in death, and life is at hand in our minds, hearts, and lives. If you can let go of what you want, if you look for money, or if you look for a wife, you will not find peace unless it comes from Christ. Look for His plan and will to give you peace, then joy is yours forever. The kingdom of God is at hand in our hearts, minds, and lives. You can do all things through Christ who strengthens you. You can be all that Christ made you. You can find love in Christ to give to others. You can be the father to your Children that Christ gives. You can be the friend to the lost in His church who can't find peace. You can be only what Christ made you to be. Find His plan, and you can and will be your life story. You can be all that Christ made you. Put up the King of Kings, and you can and will be your life story. Christ is at hand, and love is yours. I can see the Good Shepherd.

# Inside Us

You have to strike a balance between the spirit and the natural. Christ has given us a choice to find the hidden treasure in Him in this life. The fear of what people think and say of you will be washed away from the inside of us. If we allow the Holy Spirit in, it takes time to be washed by Christ. But in time, you will be cleaner than when you started. The only way to get rid of all sin is death. As for me, I am not ready to feel that good. So continue to let the Holy Spirit clean up your life on the inside. If a man or woman thinks or believes something that is not true in their mind and heart, it becomes reality to them. It is written that even Christ was not received in His own town. Allow the Holy Spirit to be on the inside of your life because we all miss Christ in our minds, hearts, and life at times. Find peace on the inside, and you will hear the whisper through the dark. It's what comes out of our mouths at times that takes our peace of mind.

Deal with the truth and what is going on inside of your life. It is hard to be washed By God. It can be done in one moment, or it can take a lifetime at times. In Jesus Christ, all things are possible when we allow Him inside us. The Father, Son, and Holy Spirit would like to meet you where you are today. They are always with us. It is our heart that is full of sin at times when we have been broken by a great loss in our life. Do not lose heart. We all have to wait on Christ. Stand still, and find peace, hope, and love in yourself. That is Christ inside you. All good in you and this world is His. And you are wrapped around His goodness. The Holy Spirit is in you today. This is a day of hope whether it is the valley or on the mountaintop. Christ is within you today.

# Less Is More at Times

When we build a car, we do not think the car can fly or carry the load like a semi-truck. We do not expect a high-rise building to drive you to work. When a baby is born, we know it can't walk and talk right away. So when dealing with young and broken Christians, remember all have brokenness or cardinal mind in some ways. We must use great patience. Less is more until Christ changes you and them.

God made us all with different gifts. When we lose our peace, we usually are focused on something we can't change in ourselves or something in someone else, or we try to be some person that God does not make us to be yet. Less is more. Be yourself today. If you do not know what Christ expects of you today, less is more. Love more, and sin less. Be yourself with in His living word, and less pain and more joy are on the way. Less is more at times. You are in Christ so more of Him and less of us today. And less will be more, and more will be less in Christ today.

# *Let's Camp*

As we go camping, we pack all the things we need. But as a child, we do not even worry about one responsibility. So what camp are you going to be in today? Christ or the devil? We can only camp in one or two spots in our spirit and life. So camp in the place where the living water of Christ is; where peace, hope, and love grow like trees; where the sunrise and sunset are perfect each day; and where the food is provided, and all the expenses have been paid by Christ. This is when we stay in His camp in our heart, mind, and life. Just camp where Jesus is. So where would you like to camp today? As for me, I sometimes find myself at the wrong campsite in my mind and life. Sin is the same in your mind and action. There are just different consequences in Christ. Do not leave his campsite today, and if you see me outside His campsite, restore me. We need each other to stay in His camp. Let's camp together today. Christ is the master camper within our life and mind.

# Let's Get Promoted

P romotion in our life will come. If we truly learn how to serve our fellow men and women within God's will for our life and theirs. Promotion is coming. Self-control, peace, and love are the fruits of true promotion. If we decide to work all of our life up the corporate ladder but do not have love, peace, and self-control in our mind, heart, and action, we truly have never been promoted. So wherever you are, seek after true promotion. Do not compromise Christ for money, sin of the flesh, or someone's opinion of you. Let Him form your understanding of true promotion. Do not lose any more chances at true promotion. If you understand this, you have been promoted, and Christ is with you. Know the Lord redeems all things for good in time. Let's get promoted.

# Living Water

━━━━━━━━━━◇━━━━━━━━━━

When I was a child, I spoke like a child. When I became a man, I put off childish things. As we grow, let the living water find you in your mind, heart, and life. So what well are you drawing from? The one that gives you confusion, disappointment, and heartache in your mind, heart, and life? Peace. Christ leaves with you not as the world gives. He gives freely to all. Christ is not a respecter of mankind or how you see yourself. The living water is within your mind, so look for the well that never runs dry with hope, peace, and love. If we make our bed in hell, He is there. So whatever you have done or wherever you are, Christ is with you. He is the air that you breathe, the hope you will find in yourself and others. That is the living well that never runs dry.

You can find and hold the peace and hope within this well of life and death. Meditate on things that are good, and whole and of things He has done for you in this life. The living water well will not run dry. All hopes and dreams come from Him, and you hold with the living water of Christ. So when you fall, we all fall. So let's live in a place where the water will not run dry. Do not try to understand everything. Have faith that Christ is pure drinking water. Just as you have faith to drink the water that comes from your tap or out of a bottle, you do not check the contents. You just have faith and drink. So faith is easy, and his yoke is light. Drink of the living water of faith. Do not drink the polluted water of sin in your mind, heart, and life. We must hold His loving or living water in our day and month and year even when we do not understand the living water of Christ at times. You are right where the Lord needs you, and do not put your faith in yourself. Hope is at hand.

# Loss and Gain

Just as one day goes, the sun rises for someone else. Just as some people pass away, the family and friends feel a great loss, and there is gain in heaven. A saint is home or out of this sinful body. There are winners and losers in the games we play. It's not hard to see the winner has gained and the loser has lost. So when we win or have great gain in this life, we must remember to think of others who have lost or don't have the same opportunities.

If I am four feet tall and sixty-eight pounds, I know that the NFL will not be calling me yet. We all have limitations, and just as every football player in the NFL had to grow past four feet tall and sixty-eight pounds, God is growing you. With Christ, all things are possible. We are all made with limitations that we and Christ can only overcome. This world builds up people who have no understanding of Christ. Do not follow them. They need you to find Christ, and you need them to pay your bills at times.

Just find true gain and loss today. This world is dying, and we all need to find a way off, and the only way off is through Christ. This world and our life are temporary. No one will make it off alive. So gain Christ and lose yourself, and you will know true loss and gain. Lose sin, and gain peace. Lose self-control, and gain stress. So today, lose unforgiving or bitterness, and you will gain peace, joy, and self-control. You will know true gain and loss as Christ sees it. We will all stand before the Father, and every knee will bow. So find true loss and gain as each day passes.

# Mail Is on the Way

Just as we send things back and forth in the mail, so does Christ. Just as you can see the mailman coming down the road, the devil can see the Holy Spirit and the angels of the Lord coming to us to deliver the letters of the Lord. Just as you can see the birds, trees, and all the things of this world, there is also a spirit world out of our perception. Just as there are wars on this earth, there are wars going on in the spiritual world, and Christ has won the wars. All we have to do is pray in all things, and do not let the devil steal your mail or the words from Christ.

Some mail gets lost, and it takes time to get there. Do not give up on the mail of Christ. He's never early. He's never late. Nothing can be held back from our God. His mail will never return to Him void just like it takes time for a package to go from California to Tennessee. Some of God's mails or increases take time to be delivered. Sometimes we are not home or not ready to receive the packages that the Lord has for us.

# *Part 2*

The mail is on the way. Do not lose hope just because it's delayed. There are principles in heaven just as on earth. Christ is a God of consistency in how He makes things. Just remember we are His packages or building blocks. Allow Christ and the Holy Spirit to build your understanding and life, then the mail will not be lost. The Lord can find all packages that have been lost, so do not lose hope in our mailman. Christ is on the way to your life and home. So what kind of mail have you been ordering in your life?

If you give hope, hope will be mailed back to you. If you give kindness, kindness is on the way. Your mailman is Christ, so make sure you are mailing the good news to all who will hear or receive Christ in your world. The mail is on the way. Hope, faith, and love are packages for you and for all. So give the package of Christ, and the mail will never be lost in life or death. We are the most valuable package. So make sure to treat everybody as a package that is fragile and valuable. We will get to know our mailman, the Holy Spirit and Christ, and then the Father, the master mailman to all. Who will receive the mailman, Christ?

# *Compromise*

There are many ways to find Christ. We think that if we go to church on Wednesday or twice on Sunday or give 10 percent of our money, we must have found religion or God. But on Monday, we go to work and think we need to fit in or stand out, and we compromise with the girls or boys to fit in or stand out. As we drive home, we tailgate or cut people off. It's okay. I went to church on Sunday.

Christ desires not just an outward appearance but a living sacrifice. In the new covenant, He wants the inner woman or man, not just the outward appearance. Now it is good to go to church and give of your money and time if they are teaching you to love Christ and all His people; denominations of the Father, Son, and Holy Spirit; and the only way to heaven is through Christ. We must not compromise God's values because others see differently or understand the word of Christ incorrectly. We all need to get to heaven. Do not let their sin bring you into being judgmental. Then you will be in the same place in your mind as they are in their action. Always remember sin in our mind and action is the same to Christ. It just does not carry the same consequence in man's eyes. So if you compromise in your mind, heart, and life, then we all lose. So compromise less, and hold the Holy Spirit more. And if you think I am or someone you know is compromising, please pray for us so we can compromise less. And we can then hold Christ together.

# Melt Like a Candle

Stir up the gifts that are within you. For your sunsets or sunrises are coming. Your God has the cosmos as His playground, and the stars are His stepping stones. Do not be ashamed of your past. You are cleansed by His work at the cross. Fear is melting away like a candle, burning throughout the night. There will be no form of fear left to control you. It will melt away. Just as snow melts in the spring, Christ will melt your heart with His. You will know holiness as He intended in the Garden of Eden. Allow the flame of Christ to find you where you are. Do not hide from Him anymore with your mind, heart, and life like Adam and Eve did. He is melting you so you and Christ can become one candle this night. So melt like a candle, and His love will find you where you are.

# My Father's House

Prepare the way of the Lord. Make your path straight. Control is only good if you're getting what you want, but it is a trap. We must learn to let go of control. Trust is better. Control is a form of fear to me at times. Then I stand still and allow the peace of Christ to find me and take back over because I have hope in Christ. Just hold on to the things He has done and shown you. It is written, "A double-minded person loses their way easy." Fall back on the life lessons He has done for us all until He reveals the beauty of where you are and makes the crooked places straight for you. Just like what He did for all the mighty women and men of His living word, you are a living mighty man or woman of God.

# Part 2

Now Christ is not in a lie. The only thing He can't do is sin. It's written, "He redeems all thing for good to you who are in his purpose." Some people say all things happen for a reason. Now I know a lie when I hear one. It does not sit well with the spirit of Christ. Christ is a God of choice, not of control. He will not make you drink and drive. Tell a lie. It is written, "The works of His hands He puts in our hands." So it's up to us in part to do well in Christ-centered living. When people fall short or make big mistakes, as we all do, Christ has us covered on earth, and the Father has us covered in heaven through Christ. So when we lose someone or something to a bad choice, that is something out of our control. All good is in Christ. Nothing is truly gone. Our perspective has been broken, so hold on to Christ. The best is yet to come.

# My Love

As I hear the word of Christ, it makes my life filled with hope, then I jump for joy. As I wait on Him who makes the sinners clean, He shows me my heart and breaks me in His hands to clean my mind, heart, and actions. There are five kinds of love in the word of God that we used for the word *love*, and we have one word in English. So sometimes, the meaning can be lost in English. The Father's love is like the cosmos. It goes on forever, but there is no air to breathe, so we must have Him to keep us safe in this world. He is the air we breathe and the hope in death and life. "I am who I am." Let's not make God in our image, then you will hear him whispering back in the dark of our mind, heart, and life. True hope and love are yours in Christ today.

# *New Christmas Tradition*

Christmas can be a great time of the year to reflect on all our wonderful blessings, or it can be a great torment if we can only see the things we do not have. If we make it about money or about us, we have lost Christmas. Let's make a new Christmas tradition. Let's find the lost ones and restore them to Christ, for the greatest gift you can give is Jesus Christ. Allow yourself to be a living sacrifice. Restore the love you have for Him, and you will start a new Christmas tradition. Then you and Christ will light up the Christmas tree of life together. Now that is a new Christmas tradition that I will take part in.

# New Life

Just as new life is born, it needs love and tenderness. When you start a relationship, it's like a seed. It needs water, sun, and clouds. Give it too much of one thing, and it will kill it. Give it too little, and it will die. The narrow road is hard to stay on in this life. That is why we need Christ and need to pray and go slow in this life. By this, you will find contentment in the place you are and who you are. Christ formed your mind and heart before the foundation of the world. If you look at all the rock formations and see how incomplete or uneven they are, it took a lot of heat and pressure to make them so beautiful. God's idea of perfect and our idea are different.

He sees your brokenness as a whole in Christ. Put a light in a vase with cracks and holes in a dark room and see how beautiful each crack is. God loves you in your shattered places, and He will find you and make you shine. Just as Cain and Abel gave their gifts to God. Always give your best. Cain gave something of no value. In his own heart, it's not just about money, time, church, or family. It's about you and Christ. Remember to give your life. He needs you as much as you need Him. If you will not praise Him, the rocks will cry out. His word will not return to Him void. Your new life starts each day. Do not look back in regret. Only look back to remember where Christ Has led you out of. New life is in Christ today.

2 Corinthians 5:17–18

# Only One Religion

There are many denominations and churches that believe in the Father, Son, and Holy Spirit. I know there is only one God—Christ the Lord. His desire is to not lose one soul to hell. Hell was created for the angle of darkness. Blasphemy or denying Christ is the only way to hell. It's the one thing that will keep you from Him. So love or act like everyone that you run into has something you want—friendship, money, or whatever drives you. What I am saying is that we can walk in love. But it is hard to do with someone you think you need nothing from. But they need you to find Christ, and you need them to see yourself. So look for peace and love and self-control in yourself. Then you will be able to give it to others because Christ gives freely, and so should we. Build on the foundation of love. Remember there is only one unforgivable sin—denying Christ. If someone is in sin and all are, act like they have something you want or need until God teaches us deeper love. The only religion in heaven and in this world is Christ Jesus our Lord.

Galatians 1:8–10

# Our Heart

―――――――――――――――

When you look for joy, you will see it. When you look for peace, it is there. What we see is our heart looking back at us, not always the truth. If you can see the good in someone or yourself, focus on that. If you see brokenness, then all have brokenness. Always go to Christ. He is able to help them or show you how to help. If you're getting into any type of relationship, look out for a friend who looks out for you and tries to understand your heart the way the Father has made you. If you look outward, Christ will fill you on the inside of your life.

It's okay to be hurt. It's okay to be sad. It's part of sin in this life without Christ. If you do not open up to Christ, you will truly miss out on this life. Just remember that do not open yourself up to people who think of themselves first. Find Christ-centered people who cover you in love and peace and who speak the truth. Always read God's living word like a child, and you will see Him as He sees you. Make your heart His today.

# Peace, Hope, Love

Finding God is hard at times. Finding love and hope is where the Lord is. So find peace in yourself and hope in life then you will start to know Christ. The Lord gives hope and peace in the storms of life. All peace, hope, and love that cover your mind and heart are Christ within your life. All good is from Christ. All confusion is from you or the devil. God gives you a spirit of peace, hope, and love. So pray in all things. He is peace, hope, and love so always read His living word with love, hope, and peace toward you and others. Then you will see love, peace, and hope, whispering back to you in his word. "I am who I am." Let God be God and you be you. Then you will hold Him wherever life is. Now Christ is with you. It is our heart that cannot see at times. Peace, hope, and love are Jesus Christ in us all. Give it to others each day, or find someone to give it to you. And you will have Christ with you. Peace, hope, and love.

1 Corinthians 13

# Pinball

I am like a pinball in a pinball machine. It seems like I am going nowhere, bouncing around, but then the Lord allows me to fall into His tender hands; and I look up at the scoreboard and am amazed at the change in my mind, heart, then my life. So do not despise small beginnings. You are in the pinball machine of your life at times, so hold the Father, Son, and Holy Spirit and your three pinballs will never run out. There is freedom in the pinball machine of life; just hold Christ, and your score will light up this world and your life.

# *Preacher*

Time for joy, time for peace, time to understand, and time to have faith. There is always time to let the Holy Spirit lead us into His preaching. Only Christ truly knows what each person needs each day. So go to the master preacher today. He is the preacher within you. We must be led by the Holy Spirit and not by man's understanding of the living word of Christ. Preach His song, and you will be a preacher of His will. Just be as simple as Jesus. So we do not become too spiritual that we preach a message to people who cannot hear or understand. His hidden wisdom is within you if you hold onto Christ. Be yourself within God's living word. Whether you are a great thinker, a great listener, or a great teacher, we are all great at something in Christ. We all have different gifts, so be the preacher of your gifts from Christ. The preacher will be seen, and the master preacher (Jesus Christ) will teach us all.

True preach is Christ within all preachers.

James 3:7–12

# *Put Yourself on Top*

The first will be last, and the last will be first. It's better to give than to receive. These words are from the living word of Christ. So put yourself on top by looking out for your family and friends through God's eyes. First, we must put His teachings in our minds to allow Him to be in our hearts. So we can truly understand His word in His image in our life. If we continue to drive the wrong way on a one-way street, there are going to be problems, so be careful with one-way relationships, or you will get run over in your mind and life. That is if you do not set for yourself boundaries in your mind and actions. So put yourself on top by laying down your life, and picking up His yoke is easy. Just don't lay down something you are not ready to let go of. It will torment your mind. Seek Christ, and give your best with common sense within His living word. Now put yourself on top, and lay down your will today. Christ is a God of choice, not control. So put yourself on top.

2 Timothy 1:6–7

# See It Through

If we put too much emphasis on where we are or where somebody else is, it will take our peace that comes from Christ even if they're not where they should be. Let go, or hold on and let God do the work in you. So you can have the peace from Christ to see it through. It's a two-edged sword, and no man or woman can understand what is truly going on in the hearts of mankind at times. If we hold the scriptures in our own minds, without God's revelation, we will miss out on their meaning. We can read a scripture ten times and get ten different meanings. The Holy Spirit is the translator so we do not lose the meaning of what Christ is teaching. We are alive, and His word is too. God's ways are as far as heaven is from the earth. Go slow, and the fruit of the Holy Spirit will overflow in your life. Let Him build your understanding in His living word of Christ, and only Christ and you can see it through. Run to our Father, and you will see it through each day of your life.

Philippians 2:1–4

# Sin Is a Wind

S in is like a wind in my mind at times. It seems to come and go as it wills, but I know Christ is in control of the wind of my mind. Christ pours His understanding in the wind, so the wind will not overtake me. As the wind blows, I will not be moved. Christ is the storm of hope, peace, and self-control. We are all in the wind of sin in our minds. Our hope is in Christ, not in our understanding but in His. As sin comes, the Lord will rise up a tide that will sink all ships of sin in our minds. Just hold on to the wind of peace, hope, and self-control; and the sin will not overtake you. My sin is running down the cross of Calvary. Your wind of sin will not overtake you. Hold the wind of peace, hope, and love. The sin will not reach your heart in Christ. Hope is at hand, and the wind of sin is at bay.

# Singing in Tune

A s each word the Lord speaks, it rains from heaven; and the sound of hope, peace, and self-control will overtake your heart and life. Allow each word to overtake your mind in love toward others and yourself. Sing in tune by staying out of the Holy Spirit's way in your words and action. You can do all things in Christ who strengthens you. When we struggle to carry the correct note or sing in tune, do not destroy ourselves by accusing others or ourselves. You hold Christ, then you can sing in tune. Just sing the song that Christ puts in your Heart. If its kindness, patience, or hope, sing in tune, and you will hold Christ; and the song will ring down through the ages. Sing your song to Christ, and He will sing it too all from your mouth, and you are in tune with Him. Sing to Christ, and He will part your seas and make your crooked places straight as He sings in tune. So hold the master note maker, and the song will be in tune.

Philippians 2:14–18

# *Stay Green*

I f we start a fire to get kindling and woods that are dried out, those
drier are better, starting with the twigs and dead branches. That is
how the devil tries to start a fire through young Christians or the ones
who think they know Christ but do not hold love, or have hidden
rotten branches on the inside of their heart and have not repented or
turned from their ways. It can be a tree that is one year old or a tree
that's 120 years old. All trees can and will be burned if they do not
stay in Christ. The church with two or the church with ten thousand.
Keep your tree in Christ so that you do not dry out. Just as the Lord
says, "If a branch is dead throw it in the fire, but if you take a green
branch it will not burn as easy." The devil wants to dry you out and
destroy you.

First, he tries to take you off the tree by pulling you from
church, your calling, or family and friends so he can burn you. Then
he tries to dry you out in your mind: "You're fat, you're no good, and
you can't do right." He tries to get you off the tree that is Christ so
He can dry you out. Remember Jesus Christ is the moisture within
your branches in life. Stay green in your life, then the devil will have
a hard time starting a fire. Just as the fire of sin burns in this world,
then there are only ashes left in people's lives, Christ will take our
ashes and give us beauty. Christ can redeem all things for good to
those who are called according to His purpose. Stay green, and the
devil will have a hard time starting a fire in your life.

Timothy 5:12–16

# Steal and Destroy

The devil comes to steal and destroy our unity in Christ. Do not allow the Holy living word of God to be twisted and to let love, hope, and self-control be lost by religious rules and laws of mankind's understanding. They only know the surface of the living word of God (Mam's milk). Remember we are made in his image and likeness. Christ has a sense of humor. If we lose a joyful heart and try to put Christ in our sinful image, we have lost Christ in our self. If our love starts to accept sin as truth, then we have lost love, and we have lost Christ in His understanding. Hold onto truth, not sin. In Christ, we will see. If something is sin, wait for Christ and the Holy Spirit to show you how to plant and water without destroying unity. The Lord came to this world not to condemn us but to give us life, hope, and truth in His ways. So bring hope and peace to the sinners as we all are. And the devil or the devil of our own mind will have a hard time stealing and destroying our minds and lives in Christ.

1 Corinthians 2: 11–16

# Still a Child in My Father's House

I am still a boy in my Father's eyes as the years pass and the decades fly by. I am still a boy in the Father's house. Always find the child within your heart and mind, and you will enter the kingdom of Christ in the Father's house. So do not lose your inner child no matter if you're 13 or 115. We must be a child in the Father's house. Christ will never stop searching for that childlike faith in your heart and mind to give you hope, peace, and joy. We are all children in the Father's house. As we grow in the Holy Spirit, we are still His baby girl or boy in our Father's eyes. Only Christ in your life can bring the increase in your heart, mind, and life. Why do we hide ourselves from Christ? So trust my words. You are in the Father's heart. Allow Christ to form your life. He is slow to show himself to us at times. He is who He is, so do not let your heart be troubled. You are with the one who puts the stars in the heavens and knows the number of hairs on your head. Always remember Christ is the doorway to the Father's house. Christ is within your mind and life through the Holy Spirit. Just be a child in the Father's house, then you will find contentment as a child in the Father's house.

1 Corinthians 2:9

# Stillness

When the water of life is calm, we can see our reflection in Christ. When the tornado is formed, it creates great destruction. But in the eye of the tornado, there is stillness. Just as Christ is the stillness of our storms, find the eye of the tornado, and stillness is yours. The Lord never promised us that the storms would not come. Only that we can find peace. So run to the eye of your storm, and the peace of Christ is yours, and you will not be destroyed just like the works of our flesh. Hope will be found in the aftermath because He saved you. The most important thing is that we must not put all of our worth in earthly things. Our true hope is in Christ and in the will of our Father who is in heaven. Find stillness in the Holy Spirit, and you will be with Christ in this life. Pour your life out as a living sacrifice, and He will pour out stillness in the eye of your storm. His yoke is easy. Do not overwork yourself in Christ. Strike a balance where He wants you. Christ is large enough to create this world and small enough to fit inside your heart, mind, and life. So be still today, and the stillness of Christ is at hand.

# *Sunrays*

J oy is on the sunrays of each day. Hold the sunrays from the sun, and you are holding Christ. As the sun comes down on your face, know that it's His Love on a cold day, warming your face. If the sun of this world moves too far away, we will not live. So hold the true Son of God of this world, and you will never taste death. Only see the wicked fall, and if we do our part, not one will be wicked. Christ's will is not to lose one person to the lies of this age. His hope is alive in you who believe. So hold fast to love, and hold fast to the sunrays of Christ. Love is on the way to the wicked, and they will know the hope that we know, and joy will be in their hearts with us all. If we destroy the wicked, we destroy ourselves. Do not give up on them. Love is the sunrays they need to find Christ, and we need to hold if we are true Christ's followers. Do not let the wicked fall. If they fall, then we all fall. We are the sunrays that people can hold, so be good and be of good cheer. Christ is riding on the sunrays each morning.

# The Fish

S almon have to swim upstream to lay their eggs, and then they
die. In this life, to do the right things, we must swim upstream to
be morally pleasing to God. So truth can be planted in the heart of
this dark world, who thinks of themselves first. So what kind of fish
are you today? As for me, I am tired of trying to please this world.
We need to lay our life down and pick up His cross so we can swim
upstream. We must learn to sacrifice our sinful desires. So we can
hold the works of our Father who created us. So what kind of fish are
you in your fishbowl today? And if you see someone out of the water,
make sure you put them back in. Do not cause your brother or sister
to stumble or stay out of the living water of Christ. Just put them
back in the water, and peace is yours, and hope for them is at hand.
Christ is the great white within the living water of this life.

Romans 4:17–21

# The Flame of Christ

The Lord is the flame that keeps this world from imploding on itself, as each day comes and goes. If you keep the flame of Christ in your mind and heart, you will not be destroyed. In the desert of your own wilderness, hold fast to Jesus Christ. King David, Mary, Peter, Queen Esther, and all the mighty men and women of Gods' living word are alive in us today. With the same word, love will lead you from the desert to the kingdom of joy, hope, and contentment. In where you have been, where you are, and where you going, Christ can only bring the increase in our life and others; and He is within you. Always work on the small things to keep your path straight. Each day has its own wilderness. So stay close to the flame of Christ. As James, the mighty man of God, says, "Faith without works, kindness, long suffering in His word" (James 2:14, 19). Now that is holding the flame of Christ today. Then the flame will just burn up all our sin and worldly desires within our life when we hold the flame of Christ.

# The Flame Is Hot
# The Master Key

For there are many locks and different combinations to open safes and doors. There are hundreds and thousands of different keys and combinations in this world. But the only key that can unlock eternity is Jesus Christ. He is the master key. He is the only key that can unlock heavenly doors and earthly doors. He is the master locksmith. Christ can make algebra or calculus as easy as one plus one. His master key or commandment is to love one another as He has loved us. The key to unlocking heavenly doors is faith, and faith comes from hearing Christ.

God's idea of faith can be as simple as believing that He dies for our sin. Faith doesn't have to be some kind of magical potion or a fifty-step program. It is as simple as hearing and doing just as giving your friend in trouble a means of escape. Just remember the master key or combination is to be slow to speak and quick to listen, and in that time, the Lord will give you the words to speak. Just as he spoke to Mary, Moses, Jacob, Queen Esther, Paul, and all the mighty men and women of His living word. For the Lord is not a respecter of persons. His laws are just like gravity, for they are set in order. For if you give, it shall be given to you. If you throw a ball up, it will come back down. For these are the principles that the Lord has set in order since the beginning of time. For the world says there are many combinations and keys to be truly successful. But the only true success that matters is that we please our creator who is in heaven and to love one another as He has loved us. That is the master key to this life. Love covers a multitude of failures and mistakes caused by sin. So go to the master key maker, Christ, today.

John 5:11–14

# The Mind

When you start something new, your mind will be put to test. If you have been doing the same thing over and over in your mind, heart, and life, you get worn out. In His time, we will understand if we hold love for one another. We do not have to be right all the time. Just hold love, hope, peace, and self-control to yourself and to others; and the mind will slow down. Do not go somewhere you lose your peace in Christ. All peace is Him and in you, and do not go somewhere with your mind and heart 'cause your words will follow. It will take your actions down the wrong road. Where your mind is, your body, mouth, and actions will go.

We are all in one body in Christ. So take captive every thought, and hear the Lord speak. He brings hope, love, and peace in your mind. It's time to put the living word to work in your mind, and your life will get better. We are all the same in Christ. So hold the hope in Christ in the darkness of your mind, and the Lord will make the crooked places straight. His love is sufficient in your weakness, in your mind, in your actions, and in your life. Fear not. The Father, Son, and the Holy Spirit created all the things you can see. If you take a telescope and gaze into the heavens, they go forever. There is no end in His understanding in our minds. The only thoughts we can hold in our mind are good thoughts to others and ourselves, and Christ will find us with peace, and He will love us just a little more in our mind and thoughts upon the thoughts He is adding.

Where the mind goes, the body will follow. So hold love in your mind and to yourself and others, and make sure to stay with people who give you good thoughts. If the mind is not good, our words will be death to us all. So let your mind rest, and Christ will find you in your mind. Hope is in Christ, not how good we did today. Hold love in your mind, and you will sleep in peace.

# The Game

S in in your mind is the same as an outward sin to God. The difference is that there are different consequences for walking in it or for thinking about it. All sins are taken us away from the presence of the Holy Spirit. That brings death to our life and death to our family and friends. Hold love when your spiritual eyes are blinded by your sin or someone else's until He leads you to peace in yourself, so you do not fall into more sin. We are all the same. We need Christ to have joy, peace, and understanding. We are all workers in the field of Christ. The first one and the last one will receive the same reward of everlasting life in Christ. We are all the same. Let's stand and fall together. We are all the same. We will rise from the ashes together. We are all the same. Hold your neighbor as yourself. We are all the same when we find Christ.

# The Things We Hide

If you value something, you put it in a safe spot. So as we walk with Christ, put Him in your heart, mind, and life. If you hide sin in your mind, heart, and life from Christ, you are denying the waymaker to protects your hidden treasure. So what are you hiding from? If we deny the galaxy maker, we will never see our hidden potential and future in Christ. Just remember to hide yourself in Christ and people who think of Christ and you first. Your past is truly going to become your past in Christ, and your past will never affect you again if you do not hide from Him each day.

The things we hide are the things that torment us at times. It's not up to you to bring the power of Christ. It's Him in you. Just be you today, and the hidden things will be washed away. And then we will see the hidden things in Christ. You have never been outside of the presents of Christ. He is the air you breathe, and all our hopes are from Him. It is our heart, not His. If you make your bed in hell, He is with you. Nothing is lost if you hold Christ in the hidden places. And if you are looking for Him, He will always be with you. Our sin just blinds us at times. You are in the hidden place with Christ. You are wonderfully and beautifully made in His image just where you are.

# The Voices

There are many voices crying out. There are many thoughts and perspectives in this world that think they are right and even willing to die for that voice. The only voice that brings life is Jesus Christ. So what voices are you hearing today? Are you seeing the truth or your own heart? We must compare our thoughts to those of God's word, and make the voice of Christ leads us by His peace. Do not stray from the voice of God today, and you will achieve peace and hope in life even when there is a great loss. The voice is crying out in your wilderness. Make the way straight for the Lord in your heart, mind, and life; and His voice will find you with peace, love, and self-control. Let go of your voices, and hold His. Christ is not the accusing voice in our minds and life. He did not even accuse the women caught in the very act of adultery. So what voice are you speaking with today? Do not stone the ones who are in sin, or stone yourself today. The Lord loves you with His voice, and He wants you to love with your voice.

Hear His Voice Then Act

John 4:48–51

# The Wind of New Beginnings

When we start something new, we must go slowly. We start at the beginning of the Lord teaching us. If we go too fast, we will go right past His peace and joy, for each day we must not get in front of Christ in the natural. We are all children in this life especially when the Lord gives you a new word. Do not fight the wind of change in Christ or another way to look at it. Do not keep going around the mountain the same way. Go the new way over the mountain. God knows the best way through the crooked places. We must master stillness in Christ before He moves us. If we cannot see the Lord's peace, how can we move? Peace is what He left with us, not as the world gives. So still your mind and heart in the place where you are. Christ is the waymaker of each day. Why did you think Christ bears our iniquities? So that we can walk, not run. You can bear fruit in season and out of season. If you hold stillness and boldness, do not try to bring increase or control people. They are like the wind. They will go where they please as you learn to submit to the Lord's peace. The wind of new beginnings will be still. If we truly believe that Christ created the world in six days, why do we try to control the wind?

# Time to Know

We know the trees and the birds are God's wonderful words made for us. His word is like the wind of this world. It has great power. So make sure you are in the wind and not fighting the storm of Christ. Let Him have control. There is no peace in Christ when you are in control. It is time to know you are right where God is. If we make our bed in hell or in heaven, He is with us. Do not fear your bad choices, you're not alone. Give your understanding to Christ, and He will relight your heart, mind, and peace. It's time to know. Who can stop the will of our Father? Who is in your heart? Do not try to take over. Hold peace in Christ when life is hard. Eat the words of our Father, and the living God will find you. It is time to know. Do not listen to the devil. Listen to Christ, the one who knows all things. I am in control if you cannot see. Just hold my living word, and peace I will send to you. Is he the one who knows and is in control, or is your knowledge leading you? Let the prince of peace find you, and you will know, and joy is in our hearts.

# Trying to Understand His Word

The reason why God sometimes separate's the powerful men and women of Christ is to separate them from the culture of this age or world for a time, so he can shape them. Do not run from how you feel. Run to Christ, and embrace yourself to see Him in you. We do not define God's living word and His meaning by our understanding but by His grace. So if we know God's word in our mind, then in time, we can understand His meaning. Our understanding of His word is as far as the east is from the west at times. Only Christ can give you the truth of His word. His ways lead to life. Our ways lead to confusion with no fruit in our life. Another life lesson in our mind or life is to trust Christ.

Let's say that a man speaks God's word of healing, and the power of the Holy Spirit does not come. We know he or she is speaking God's word outside of His will or meaning. It is written that God redeems all things for good to those who are called according to his purpose. So make sure to redeem others when they're outside of God's purpose. Love covers a multitude of our lost understanding of His word. Bring life to all if you have the heart to hear Christ crying out for all to come. His desire is not to lose one to hell. And if you hold love and Christ, you will understand his word today. Hold His understanding in your mind and life.

John 4:31–35

# Where He Is I Would Like to Be

One thing I have learned in part is that it steals our peace. Even if it's wrong or not, it still has to be about me in part. Jesus was able to control Himself and bear our iniquities. So always read His word with love and hope like a child accepting it by faith. As our culture and own minds say, "it's all about you." Only Christ can truly clean our hearts by bringing our sin in the open or out of the closet of our mind and life because true peace comes from being in Christ. We can search the world over with only our self and never see true peace. That's why the world can't understand. They see peace as just getting what they want as did I. So if you truly want to make it all about yourself, give yourself to Christ, and He will give you to others. Where Christ is, there you will be.

John 3:29

# *Wisdom*

All good things come from Christ. All confusion, sin, deception, and death come from not being in God's perfect plan. Now we have no chance to get back to the garden of Eden without the Father, Son, and Holy Spirit. Now we have to serve Him in this broken world. Love is the only wisdom we need. Love one another by using common sense, seeing the truth in God's living word in where you are and how to love each other. Sometimes love or wisdom is to let go. We have to be led by the Holy Spirit, and it will be confirmed two or more times. Then we have to have faith to walk in God's word. It will bear the fruit that God wants. It's not always our desire, but in time, we usually will understand if we have love and wisdom for one another. When we have wisdom and no love, we have nothing. So hold wisdom in this life and all do. Give wisdom in love, and you will lead them to Christ, or you will find Christ for yourself. If we have wisdom and love, then we can hold the works of His hands—hope, peace, and healing of all kinds. They are on the way. Hold love and wisdom for one another.

Wisdom
John 1:8–13

Common Sense
John 3:17–21

# David Edward Lorang

I was born in 1981, and I was one of three and the only one who was planned. I had a hard time fitting in with school. I had a hard time reading and writing, and I had no confidence in myself because I couldn't do a simple task that teachers required of me as a child and teenager. When I was fifteen, I started to drink alcohol and smoke weed to deal with the anxiety I didn't know I had. Now how did a fifteen-year-old get alcohol? A party store started to sell me hard liquor and beer, and I thought it was the coolest thing. How wrong was I? Let's just say I struggled from the seventh through the eleventh grade, trying to fit in, and the harder I tried, the more people didn't like me.

I decided to go on a trip that changed my whole life with some kids I've never really got to know. I know I got drugged for about a week with LSD. Then my mind was never the same. I spent two weeks in a hospital, and I asked God that if He would restore my mind, I would give Him my life. He did, and it was amazing and scary to know Christ is real. I had plans to go to college; and all things change in my heart, mind, and life. This book is about how Christ teaches me and how to hear His love in my mind. I hope you in joy Christ in my heart and put into words. Now it's up to you to believe the truth of who I am or the label that the world puts on me. All things are possible in Christ.

# *Love Letter to My God*

For my hope in life is in your hands. No one can take you from me or me from you. We are one in you. You lifted my soul from pain and gave me peace. In my confusion, I stood still and saw your glory. No man or my own thoughts can take you from me. My love is wrapped around the cross, and my heart beats for your touch, O Lord. Come and hold my mind, heart, and life. I am a flower fading in the field. Without your covering, I would not be able to stand in this life. When I deserve rain and storms, you give me sunshine to lift me closer to you as you open my heart to your love. As the wind blows, I will not be moved. My heart is yours. For you are the small still voice I can hear now whispering back to my heart. My soul is filled with joy. Just as new life is born, my love grows to the heavens, and I see how clean you are. Pour your understanding on me so I can tell all about your love to others, so they may find the good news

# Two Masters

There is my will and God's will. My life is the will of the father who is in heaven. My mind, heart, and life are the tale of two masters—what I want and what Christ has given me. My hope is that His will in me is stronger than my own choice at times. If Christ does not hold me in His tender hands, I will not stand. I will give in to the sinful man and the will of my own. Our hope is in His power, love, and peace that pass our understanding that Christ is the two masters of my life. He mastered my sin, and He mastered my relationship with him. Christ is my gatekeeper, the one that keeps me from entering sin in my heart, mind, and actions. Lord forgives me for serving my own interest at times when I desire my will and walk in it. The desire of sin is at the door, and our will is for it. Christ is the master of my sin. He keeps me from opening the door to the will of this age. Christ is greater than our sin, and the devils will destroy us. Resist sin and the devil. Christ is in you, and Christ can do all things for His people, and all is His. Every knee will bow in heaven and earth, and my will also kneel. He is the two masters of my life, and my hope is found at the cross.

# Hear Christ

D o not turn your back to the Lord's people. Hold hope, love, and self-control, and walk in peace and love. Turn your heart from the teachings of man and hold My yoke, and love is on the way to your understanding and your words will be as Mine are in power. Do not put your understanding of doctrine ahead of Christ. I am how I am just as you would like people to like you for you. You are made in My image and likeness. Let's not put our schedule or traditions ahead of your Creator. Keep Me centered in your schedule and tradition so you do not lose Me, the One who created you from the dust of this earth. I am slow to speak, and My words are soft as the clouds in the sky and as powerful as a hurricane. I am not in the storm, the fire. I am the small still voice in your mind, heart, and life. I am all around you; the air you breathe is Me. The hope in you is Me. I am all good things. My hope is your love for one another is as strong as My love is for you. That is why I sent My only Son, Christ, to your life and you will live forever in My kingdom and your love is Me in you. So stop looking for Me. I am within you, and in your weakness, we will be made strong. Death is not the end; it is the beginning of our lives to getter in spirit and truth. We will search the star and the heavens together. You are My family, and there is nothing I will not do for you. I made you so you can hold me inside of you. We are one in Me. Hold Christ and you are holding Me. I never leave you or forsake you. Just as Satan fell like lightning from heaven, I can't wait for us to kick Satan out of our earth. When Christ comes through the clouds this earth, we'll be back in your hands. See, Christ and Satan will fall like lightning from earth and rest in hell forevermore, and we will rain on earth as it is in heaven forevermore. Hear Christ speak.

# About the Author

David Lorang was born in 1981, Oakland County, Michigan. He went to ministry school and graduated in 2006. He loves hiking and riding a bike and all outdoor sports. Photography is also one of his passions. Some of his work has been published throughout the national parks, but his biggest passion of all is for Jesus Christ and to see people find the true way to hope and prosperity.

CPSIA information can be obtained
at www.ICGtesting.com
Printed in the USA
LVHW070558080222
710536LV00010B/172